PowerKiDS
Readers

MY COMMUNITY
MI COMUNIDAD

A TRIP TO THE
FIREHOUSE

DE VISITA EN LA
ESTACIÓN DE BOMBEROS

Josie Keogh

Traducción al español: Eduardo Alamán

PowerKiDS
press™

New York

Published in 2013 by The Rosen Publishing Group, Inc.
29 East 21st Street, New York, NY 10010

First Edition

Editor: Amelie von Zumbusch
Book Design: Ashley Drago

Traducción al español: Eduardo Alamán

Photo Credits: Cover, p. 9 © Bianca Dermody; p. 5 Lawrence Migdale/Photo Researchers/Getty Images; p. 6 iStockphoto/Thinkstock; pp. 10, 14, 17, 18, 21, 24 Shutterstock.com; p. 13 Simone Mueller/Stone/Getty Images; p. 22 © www.iStockphoto.com/Debi Bishop.

Library of Congress Cataloging-in-Publication Data

Keogh, Josie.
  [Trip to the firehouse. Spanish & English]
  A trip to the firehouse = De visita en la estación de bomberos / by Josie Keogh ; translated by Eduardo Alamán. — 1st ed.
      p. cm. — (PowerKids readers. My community = Mi comunidad)
  Includes index.
  ISBN 978-1-4488-7830-7 (library binding)
  1. Fire stations—Juvenile literature. 2. Fire fighters—Juvenile literature. I. Title. II. Title: De visita en la estación de bomberos.
  TH9148.K4613 2013
  363.37'8—dc23
                              2011052881

Websites: Due to the changing nature of Internet links, PowerKids Press has developed an online list of websites related to the subject of this book. This site is updated regularly. Please use this link to access the list:
www.powerkidslinks.com/pkrc/fire/

Manufactured in the United States of America

CPSIA Compliance Information: Batch #CS12PK: For Further Information contact Rosen Publishing, New York, New York at 1-800-237-9932

CONTENTS

CONTENIDO

We went to the firehouse.

Fuimos a la estación
de bomberos.

5

Rex the dog lives there.

Rex, el perro, vive en la estación.

7

The firehouse has three
fire trucks.

La estación de bomberos
tiene tres camiones de
bomberos, llamados
autobombas.

9

Some have long ladders.

Algunos camiones tienen
escaleras muy largas.

Tim's dad is the fire chief.

El jefe de la estación es el papá de Tim.

14

The firefighters put on their gear.

Los bomberos se ponen
su equipo.

It keeps them safe from a
fire's heat.

Esto los mantiene seguros en
el calor del fuego.

17

18

There was a fire on Pine Street!

¡Hay un incendio en la calle Pine!

19

The firefighters put the fire out.

Los bomberos apagan
el incendio.

21

They saved Ana's cat!

¡Los bomberos salvaron al gato de Ana!

23

WORDS TO KNOW / PALABRAS QUE DEBES SABER

ax: A tool for cutting through things.

hacha (el): una herramienta para cortar cosas.

helmet: A covering that protects the head.

casco (el): una cubierta que protege la cabeza.

hose: A bendable tube for carrying liquids.

manguera (la): un tubo, flexible, que lleva el agua.

INDEX

ÍNDICE